EQUALITY THE FUTURE HOPE POVERTY WAR DISASTER DESTRUCTION DISCRIMINATION BULLYING POLLUTION IDENTITY POWER DREAMS

THE POWER OF POETRY

Raise Your Voice

Edited By Debbie Killingworth

First published in Great Britain in 2023 by:

 Young**Writers**

Young Writers
Remus House
Coltsfoot Drive
Peterborough
PE2 9BF
Telephone: 01733 890066
Website: www.youngwriters.co.uk

Printed and bound in the UK by BookPrintingUK
Website: www.bookprintinguk.com
YB0527P

FOREWORD

Since 1991, here at Young Writers we have celebrated the awesome power of creative writing, especially in young adults where it can serve as a vital method of expressing their emotions and views about the world around them. In every poem we see the effort and thought that each student published in this book has put into their work and by creating this anthology we hope to encourage them further with the ultimate goal of sparking a life-long love of writing.

Our latest competition for secondary school students, **The Power of Poetry,** challenged young writers to consider what was important to them and how to express that using the power of words. We wanted to give them a voice, the chance to express themselves freely and honestly, something which is so important for these young adults to feel confident and listened to. They could give an opinion, highlight an issue, consider a dilemma, impart advice or simply write about something they love. There were no restrictions on style or subject so you will find an anthology brimming with a variety of poetic styles and topics. We hope you find it as absorbing as we have.

We encourage young writers to express themselves and address subjects that matter to them, which sometimes means writing about sensitive or contentious topics. If you have been affected by any issues raised in this book, details on where to find help can be found at
www.youngwriters.co.uk/info/other/contact-lines

CONTENTS

Rachel Rankin (12)	73
Liam Cunningham (11)	74

Looe Community Academy, East Looe

Rufus Higgins (12)	75
Reid Hopkins (12)	76
Sophia Williams (12)	77
Michael Caddy (12)	78
Sophie Haywood (13)	79
Rocky Reason (12)	80
Archie Chainey-Smith (12)	81
Cerys Vickery (12)	82
Evie Pearson-Roselle (12)	83
Thurston Rich (12)	84
Zachary Underhill (12)	85
Sam Honey (12)	86
Dominic Juleff (12)	87
Brandon Sibley (12)	88
Gabriel Gutierrez (13)	89
Lilia Jackson (12)	90
Adam Courtenay (12)	91
Kara Mark (12)	92
Leah Chalk (13)	93
George Dickens (12)	94

Sybil Andrews Academy, Bury St Edmunds

Anson Wong (11)	95
Olly Ramsbottom (11)	96
George Kydd (12)	97
George Rowson (13) & Charlie	98
Aaron Baker (12)	100
Harry Fitchett (12)	101
Melisa Simsek (13)	102
Hayden-Jai Ankin (12)	103
Theo Newport (12)	104
Oscar Donoghue (11)	105
Isabelle Dyer (12)	106
Woody Gresham (12)	108
Lewie Currington (14)	109
Sienna Lionnet-Cook (11)	110

Phoebe Harden (11)	111
Freya Halls (11)	112
Megan Edley (11)	113
Charlie Hickford (11)	114
Finn Davies (11)	115
Oliver Leightley Richards (12)	116
Grace Jackson (11)	117
Merryana Bhujel (11)	118
Lilly Farkas (11)	119
Ethan Gatley (12)	120
Alfie Turner (12)	121
Rudie Lorking (13)	122
Phoebe-Mai Watts (11)	123
Joshua Hammond (13)	124
Lenny Horn (11)	125
Faith Coston (11)	126
Oliver Buerling (11)	127
Lucas Palframan (13)	128
Joe Harden (13)	129
Lauren Tee (13)	130
Zac Horler (11)	131
Isabelle Ramsbottom (11)	132
Sophie Daniel (11)	133
Layla Owen (12)	134
Marie Lebrun (11)	135
Riley Parker (12)	136
Olly Rolfe	137
Maja Wazydrag (11)	138
Poppy Moore (11)	139
Henry Heath (12)	140
William Ainger (11)	141
Ava Whelan (12)	142
Sophia Saunders (11)	143
Holly Allen (11)	144
Ollie Richardson (11)	145
Emelia Roe (12)	146
William Johnston (12)	147
Alex Robb (13)	148
Travis Hope (12)	149
Lily Cooper (11)	150
Luke Sadler (13)	151
Evie Clifford (13)	152
Alisha Moss (11)	153

Jordan Ward (13)	154
Wesley Andrade (11)	155
Rodrigo Teixeira (11)	156
Juliet Mead (13)	157
Sebine Westgate (12)	158
Louie Whiting (11)	159
Riley Wall (12)	160
Henry Myhill (11)	161
Lily Webber (12)	162
Riley Summers (11)	163
Taylor Parker (11)	164
Louie Dobbyn (11)	165
Evie Roscoe (12)	166
Erin Stewart (11)	167
Theo Baillie (11)	168
Freddie Cole (12)	169
Annie Murrell (11)	170
Aliona Day (11)	171
Sonni French (11)	172
Felix Glasscock (12)	173
Mia Dallorzo (11)	174
Oliver Bivins (11)	175
Lexie Proctor (11)	176
Franciszek Inglot (11)	177
Beau Proctor (11)	178

THE
POEMS

Always There

Blossoms elegantly drifting slowly, reaching the ground.
Walking across the light pink quilted ground,
Being cautious in attempt to preserve the unique scenery.
New life being protected like a parent protects their
children.
Coming home from school holding your mother's hand.

Warm summer's breeze hitting you like a soft touch.
Glimmering sunlight gently toasting your skin.
Birds harmonising their chirps in sync with your steps.
Your family waiting for you to get home after a day out.

A cosy blanket surrounding you with comfort and warmth.
Listening to music whilst trampling across the autumn
leaves.
The consoling crunch, stepping on each one of them.
Coming home to your mother and father,
Joy leaking out of all of you, like a dripping tap.

The winter's chill giving you goosebumps from head to toe.
All life dying, the empty trees being torn away from their
amber shield.
Rain clashing against the ground, engulfing you completely,
But your family is still there waiting for you to get home.
They are always there.

Aliza Mahmood (15)
Beaumont Leys School, Leicester

My Life

Culture is what makes me, me.
For me, it's wearing a sari
And putting on a bindi,
And speaking in Hindi;
Celebrating Diwali,
And celebrating God.

However, not all people feel the same way.
My culture is appropriated by others;
Watching them defend themselves
"We are appreciating it..."
Whilst they continue to make fun of it,
Speaking English in an 'Indian accent'
Singing songs saying
"Dot on his head, he's a..."
These racial slurs are against not only my culture
But other people's too.
And I'm supposed to believe it's being appreciated
This type of discrimination
Gets no recognition
Simply because 'it doesn't seem too deep'.

But this...
This is just the surface
The truth being our culture - our life
Is being taken like a rug

Swept from under you
And before you realise there's nothing left
And you've fallen
And still... still
People take our jewellery
Famous people use it to accessorise
But nobody will realise
What's actually going on.
The hurt they leave us with.
The world needs to realise there's a difference
Between appropriation
And appreciation.
Stealing our culture and trying to make it your own.

These problems have been covered
By a blanket;
Disguising the truth.
The truth being the reality
Of embracing your culture.
Many don't see the issue.
"We aren't discriminating your culture."
Open your eyes to this problem
You hate us for our culture and looks
But still steal it.
This is my culture -
My life.

Ria Naliyapara (15)
Beaumont Leys School, Leicester

Nostalgia

I don't know if I am a nostalgic person.
I mean in retrospect,
I do spend the majority of my time looking through old videos and photos.
But I don't know if it's because I'm nostalgic.
The definition reads a sentimental longing or wistful affection for the past
Typically for a period or place with happy, personal associations.
But I really don't know if that's what I feel.
I feel mourning.
I feel grief.
I feel aching.
Deep pains for the girl I see in those videos,
For the innocence maybe,
Or just because I won't feel it again.
I mourn for the years that have passed so suddenly,
And I cry for the present me who has to look back at videos to remember those moments.
Those feelings.
I miss the comfort of having time.
I yearn to start it all over from the very beginning,
From the second I was born.
The thing about nostalgia is that you ignore the pain you went through in-between the lines of your memories,
But I'm not leaving that out.

I want to feel it all again.
I want to go through everything all over again.
I just want one more time.
I look in the mirror and have absolutely no idea how I got here.
I miss someone I carry around every single day.
How do you continue to miss someone so deeply that you are never apart from?
How do you cope with mourning yourself?
How do you sit in your bedroom and watch videos from months or years before and not look in the mirror and astonish that you will never experience anything quite like that again?
Nostalgia is not what I live in.
A sentimental yearn is not what I feel.
I feel grief. I feel loss.

Kiera Cockram (15)
Beaumont Leys School, Leicester

Two Halves Make A Whole

Desperate solutions that have pure intentions.
Basic agreements decided and dealt with.
Christmas, birthdays and all 52 weeks are 50/50.
Communication? Unwanted and apparently unnecessary;
Because how hard can it be to pretend half of you doesn't
exist for only half of the time?

Approximately 2 miles between my DNA creation story.
History, family and 12 uneven roads is where the connection
stops.
Only 8 minutes by car but a 24/7 reminder of betrayal.
"You're going hers, she can get you!"
"You're leaving his, he can drop you!"
If I pick I'm choosing a side.

Can I have a tenner for a taxi? Please...

Wiping away tears of two undeserving 12-year-olds.
The lucky outcome of three broken hearts.
Collecting their pain and hiding it in a deep dark hole along
with mine.
Distractions dance around them, replacing the banging and
shouting upstairs.

It's not your fault; I promise.

Guilt overrides... Why? Because you've had a great day
With one and you're telling the other.
Anger devours as you sit in silence whilst they rant and
curse at you about the other.
Sadness controls because you just achieved something
great
But don't want to decide who to tell first...
Because that's choosing a side.

That's your enemy, my other parent.

Chennise Gittens (15)
Beaumont Leys School, Leicester

Guitar... A Fabulous Instrument

Guitar... A fabulous instrument
A simple riff chord progression or song and people are
in awe
Like they've been hypnotised.
However, some people don't like it
And say things like, 'Just a piece of wood with metal,
nothing amazing."
Or, "No one wants to listen," but in reality, they're probably
jealous.

Many people look up to people's success
And want to know what to do to be like them.
But you'll never listen to an instrument for advice
Because it can't talk and the only thing it can do is make
sounds
But only when it's being played, think about that.

Now listen to this, you control it just as you control your life.
You pluck a string, you make a sound
Just like when you need to scratch, you move your hand.
You play a song, you're moving all your fingers
And producing excellent sounds
Just like you're moving and talking in real life.

But one mistake and you cringe,
You messed up!
Just like in life one wrong move or word
And people start negativity about you.

Overall, you get praised like you're an angel
By most of your family, friends and strangers.
And when they ask why I started playing, well...
Guitar is a fabulous instrument!

Tomasz Gorski (15)
Beaumont Leys School, Leicester

Stop Praying...

Salty seas
From an endless reflection,
An ugly case
Harnessing the essence of stars,
And why is that magnifying glass
Only capable of focussing on your flaws?
And how is it a mirror image
But her's is better than yours?

But you're promising your sister
She's beautiful
With her diamond eyes and button nose
But she sees how you look into the mirror
With those same grey eyes,
You hate your face:
It shows.

And your insecurities bleed from you
Like an open wound,
Didn't anyone tell you
When that crimson blood spilled
Your pain's not only hurting you,
Every time you tear yourself to shreds,
You ruin their perceptions too?

Please,
Stop praying...

For him to worship you,
For her to envy you,
For them to accept you.
My love, didn't you know?
It doesn't matter if your hair's straight, wavy or curled,
It's just that beautiful things
Are so often shattered by this world.

Ruby Varney (15)

Beaumont Leys School, Leicester

A Celestial Love Story

Have you ever heard of the love story of the sun and the moon,
Who became lovers much too soon?

But one day God parted their ways,
With the impasse of night and day.

The sun, now secluded, never stops shining in the cyan sky.
Because she retains the hope to one day meet her lover and say one last goodbye.

Meanwhile, on the other side,
He hangs, empty, amidst the lonely sky

And reflects her love for him upon the world,
Where her calls for him can't be heard.

And so she grants him the gift of the stars;
For him to remember her during the dark.

And her only hope does come true
But that happens just once in a blue moon.

The sun and the moon both longing for an eclipse,
For an eclipse is a blessing they both have wished.

Now you know the love story of the sun and the moon,
Who fell for each other much too soon.

Hudha Azmy (15)
Beaumont Leys School, Leicester

Tangled

Tangled.
This feeling swallowed me up like a needle in a haystack,
Like trying to find your way to your friends in a busy crowd,
But when all these feelings get tangled
And you can't separate one from another
You accept the numbness
Because at least it acts as a cover.

Distant.
Like when you don't recognise the roads on the way home.
Like when you find yourself in an alley that's unknown
Like when you're sitting right next to them but they feel
miles away,
Like when you're slowly losing yourself day by day slowly,
You start to drift away.

Breathless.
Like when you have run too far
And you feel like it's impossible to get any air.
Like when your lungs have given out, you can't scream,
All you can do is stare,
When they don't want to help you
Because they claim life's unfair.

Lily Philpott (15)
Beaumont Leys School, Leicester

Daybreak

The sky exhales light.
Light that flows into the river,
Entangles with each branch,
Each twig,
And bleeds with the morning dew.
A crisp cue that life begets life.
And death begets living.

Winged soul
Soar and startle dawn.
Icarus.
Immortal.
Warm rain and yellow thorns.
To fly or fall
Or melt into the gold of day?
Spotlight.
Meteor.

Lead feathers
Pinched by generations undermined.
Kiss the sun, dear,
Then crash down and melt into the earth.
Asteroid.
Reborn.

'Golden child'
Reminds me more of yellow.

Churning ego, lemon heart.
Neon: greed to be seen.
Embodies light that burns too bright
Then shrivels up.

Swallow up shadows and birdsong.
Inhale ash; exhale fire.
Burn up and become the sun.
Inferno. Instinct.
Icarus.

Daybreak.

Katie Payne (15)
Beaumont Leys School, Leicester

Memories

Home;
Comfortable and safe.
Sweet-smelling candles burning
On top of the fireplace
Which gathers the ash,
The opening of the glass door
Separates the new world.

The new world becomes
Cold and empty.
Blankets of heavy clouds weigh on my shoulders
Splashing of thick rain
Floods my broken face
Like my heart
It falls
it breaks,
It...
Disappears.

Hands feel as cold as ever
Touching my pale face
Not knowing what to do.
Confused and lost.
Alone.
What? When? Why?
My memories scream in tears.

Silence.
We wrap ourselves in each other
Though we are together;
Abandoned - is what I feel.

Panic;
Memories flood back
Remembering how we used to be a pack
With laughter and jokes
And just like that
No more to be made.

I miss you!

Radhika Naran (16)
Beaumont Leys School, Leicester

Who Cares?

Walking through the street aligned with towering trees
And detached houses
Airpods in full blast,
Playlist with almost 500 songs,
Violent yet peaceful rain
Almost drowning the full-volume music, trapped in my ears,
Clothes drenched, hair dripping,
But who cares?
Because my tears are disguised
And no one really knows what I'm trying to hide...

Indian girl, long dark healthy hair,
Immersed in her culture,
Fluent in her language and compelling grades.
But that's not me.
Yes, I'm Indian and have dark hair
But it's nowhere near as long or healthy as I want it to be.

I can barely communicate with my elders,
Remember any traditions,
My mum is constantly reminding me
How detached I am from my culture
And family,
But who cares?

Sukhi Minhas (15)
Beaumont Leys School, Leicester

Family

Family is like a blanket,
Comforting you in times of need
And shielding you in times of fear.
They keep you warm
Even when you're torn.
Absorbing every little tear
Until there's no more.

However, don't be fooled,
Blankets can also keep you far too warm,
Believing it's their job to do so,
Too protecting to understand
That sometimes you need to fall into the coldest seas
To swim into the most breathtaking ocean.

Although, you should never forget
Blankets adore you despite your flaws
And love you beyond words
They intend to give a helping hand
And keep you cosy on the chilliest nights,
Forever ready to see you thrive.

Whether you fall or fly,
Your blanket's always nearby.

Kavijah Vijayananthan (15)
Beaumont Leys School, Leicester

Food

Food
Doesn't always look nice.
Doesn't always taste right.
Does however always need to be eaten.
Whether it's carbs from bread
Or protein from fish.
Whether it's your mum's, dad's
Or your favourite dish.

Food
Full of colour and flavour and life
Difficult to get to those who face strife.
Those at the top living life full and free
Know they can afford meals for you and me.
Do you think they're sitting at a dining room table
Worrying about if you are able;
To fork out the budget
To put food in your stomach?

Food
Doesn't always look nice.
Doesn't always taste right.
Does deserve to be a basic human right.
Does cause sleepless nights.

Zane Holland (16)
Beaumont Leys School, Leicester

Open Wide

You say my food takes up too much land
Yet the food for yours is at such high demand
Don't you like the taste?
Turn away and hesitate
Open wide and salivate.

You praise the apex predators we are
Yet a cow is stronger than you by far
Don't you like the taste?
Turn away and hesitate
Open wide and salivate.

You say dog meat festivals are cruel
Crates of them upon the streets of Yulin
You'll donate to a charity, you'll adopt a mule
You'll rescue the dying kitten from that bin
Is it because you can see it?
That you act as if your food isn't made from this
But you like the taste,
So you'll turn away and hesitate
Open wide and salivate.

Adele Chamberlain (15)
Beaumont Leys School, Leicester

What If?

Feminism - Gender equality;
Racism - Racial inequality;
Sexism - Sexual inequality;
Infinite eggs fall into a basket
Covering them up.
What if it didn't have to be this way?

Equality isn't something,
Something to be proud of.
It's a right.
There are chickens. There are eggs.

What if we didn't look at cases in black and white?
What if we don't judge by appearance?
What if how you're born doesn't matter?
Be proud. Be you.
There are chickens. There are eggs.

The jeers of the crowd jar me from my sleep.
A dream.
There are chickens. There are eggs.
Be brave.
Be the fox.

Dillon Barnes (15)
Beaumont Leys School, Leicester

The Passage Of Time

Chronos and Ananke
Sit hand in hand
Stretched far across the land
Perfectly at peace.
Interwoven and intertwined
Like an embracing bind
The snake-like figures were
Interlocked for all of eternity
Surpassing way beyond modernity
Perfectly at peace.
Groom and bride
Ananke, inevitability personified
Mother of fate
And Chronos, father of time
Dancing to the chime
Of the ticking clock;
Primordial and eternal
Creators: maternal and paternal
Perfectly at peace.

The ticking of the clock will not stop
Even though I have asked it politely
Why can't I be at peace
Like Chronos and his Ananke?

Piper Richardson (15)
Beaumont Leys School, Leicester

Rugby Is A Win

Rugby is a game,
A silly game some may say.
Rugby is more than just a game,
More than throwing a ball shaped like an egg.
It brings people together,
Fans sit together,
Not like in football where they sit apart.
The smells of grass,
The warmth of blankets,
The sounds of excitement,
That's what rugby's about...
Not the competition,
But the togetherness it can bring.
Rugby is a win!

Grace Baczek (15)
Beaumont Leys School, Leicester

Missed

Shoulder to shoulder,
His shooting range.
I wait, eyes shut, patient,
Excitedly anticipating the order.
Fire!
The arrows sigh out a wolf whistle as they soar.
And one by one all are hit with rose-quartz arrowheads.
All but me.
Eros admires his work, before leaving,
My head still wracked with dreams
Of coffee shop meet-cutes and rain-drenched confessions,
I was missed.

Why was I missed?

Lily Driver (15)
Beaumont Leys School, Leicester

(A)atta (B)boy

Come on you freaking traffic jam, lemme thru
I wanna college life, lemme in, lemme in
I don't care about those looks at me, I mean why should I?
It's college, it's fifteen, just give me those!

I started seeing those eyes
Like I was laughing then those kids just gave me cold stares
I just pointed at my pencil case
"Look at my superultramegafortress and joker my ace"

I gradually noticed that one shade
When I appeared in the scene there's always that cliché
They flee their gazes, flashing with my grime
I laugh with my throat choked by my crime.

They held hands on that beach,
So I went to the far end for that extra reach.
She shook it off like it was methemphatamine dust,
Others saw me coming -
Pacification bust.

I saw them.
I stayed in the shade for hours in solemn.
I reclassified my pencil case as a rat.
I am a man and not a brat.

Hands.
Held.

Hero.
Happy.

Ethan Lo (15)
Concord College, Acton Burnell

Stop Letting It Be

The glaciers melt into the sea,
Everyone being so carefree,
Sitting and letting it be.

With the sea level rising,
And the sun still shining,
Everyone being so carefree,
Sitting and letting it be.

With deforestation,
Hurting our nation,
Everyone being so carefree,
Sitting and letting it be.

With the Earth rapidly warming,
And no one responding to the warning,
Everyone being so carefree,
Sitting and letting it be.

Dumping waste in landfill,
Or not cleaning up an oil spill,
Everyone being so carefree,
Sitting and letting it be.

Letting our waste decompose forming methane,
Along with gases off the aeroplane,
Everyone being so carefree,
Sitting and letting it be.

With the carbon emission,
We should make it our mission,
To start taking action,
To stop just letting it be.

Holly Plant (15)
Concord College, Acton Burnell

Black On White

The teeth shake like a rattlesnake tail
Hissing back at me.
Making my way to the cathedra,
I sit down with my stilts wobbling.
There are always keys to be played.
Imagine how proud everyone would be
The notes mingling in the air
Travelling to the ears of the prey.

Wouldn't matter.
Wouldn't matter if everyone stares at me
Like a cat about to pounce on its prey
Waiting for it to move in the wrong way
To stare.

Pages and keys turning blank, like the removal of a black tooth.
My brain loses connection with my muscles
Like an engine trying to restart.
No hope.

Silence falls across the great hall
As all eyes are on the prey.

Sweat begins dripping to a beat and falling like notes on a page.
What should I do?
What should I do?

Anastasia Kovrova (14)
Concord College, Acton Burnell

Don't

There was a crowd of teens
In their black T-shirts
With their masks and goggles
Raising their signs
Shouting their slogans
And she was one of them

You could see the fire in her eyes
Burning with hope
Burning for her city
They were glittering like stars
Until there was a gun
Shooting right into one of them

Don't forget that sound of the shot
Don't forget that pond of blood
Don't get used to the absence of freedom
Don't succumb to the control
The fire in her eyes is still somewhere in her soul
In our souls.

Sophia Lau (14)
Concord College, Acton Burnell

Don't Ruin Your Life

Life is too precious
Life is too sweet
Life is too dangerous
Life is too scary.

Drugs are dangerous
Drugs are illegal
Drugs are scary
Drugs don't make you cool.

As I amble down the street the strong smell of marijuana
hits my face.
The smell is stronger than the power of a raging bull.
I think to myself, *it's bad, it's illegal, it's dangerous.*
The good and the bad of drugs, there's legal and illegal,
Medical and non-medical following CBD and THC.

Drugs are dangerous
Drugs are illegal
Drugs are scary
Drugs don't make you cool.

Age of 14 I try it myself.
As I ask for more and more I get more and more addicted.
I get addicted to commit a crime
I get addicted to using a substance that will and can ruin
my life.

Drugs are dangerous
Drugs are illegal
Drugs are scary
Drugs don't make you cool.

Mhairi Roy (12)
Garnock Community Campus, Glengarnock

Nuts For Netball

You need netball
To keep you happy and healthy
But if you get hurt you won't be healthy
You'll never know if you live in fear.

"It's fabulous, it's fun," they say
But my friends might not like it
Just 'cause your friends don't like something
Doesn't mean you can't pursue it.

You can meet new people, make new friends
What happens if they don't like me?
They're still a part of your team and you can't change it.

You get to compete against other people
You won't, you won't be a star netball player
You win as a team, you lose as a team
You'll never face a loss on your own.

No one's too short or tall
There will always be a spot for you
It might even make you nuts for netball.

Rhona Stuart (12)
Garnock Community Campus, Glengarnock

The Circle Of Life

Animals have a much different life than us.
Animals have to go through more stuff than us.
See animals build and survive with just their hands
While we get things handed to us with a single demand.
Some animals live just to be slaughtered and eaten
But other owners think it's right for them to be beaten.
A lot of animals in the wild have their homes destroyed,
How would you like it if your house was broken like a toy?
Now you don't understand the pain that you're causing
Because all the species die while we are all just watching.
I bet you all wouldn't like to see your friends and family
perish
Just so you can have a meal that you know you'll cherish.
At the end of the day, it's called the circle of life.
It just isn't fair that it's not a fair fight.

Ryan Allan (13)
Garnock Community Campus, Glengarnock

War

What is the point of war?
You lose a lot of people and materials
The area gets painted with corpses, bombs
And other junk from a war.
If you're really desperate for land
Attempt to negotiate for a bit of land.
War is pointless!

You might think
But they might not be willing to negotiate...
So they end up resorting to war
And plus they always clean up after the war!

They may not be willing to negotiate at that moment
That doesn't mean they aren't willing to negotiate at a later time
If they truly don't want to negotiate
Attempt to negotiate with neighbouring countries.

Even after the treaty is signed to finish the war
The war will continue for a poor farmer
Who drives his tractor over a mine...

Nikodem Kowalczyk
Garnock Community Campus, Glengarnock

I Am Only A Colour

I am only a colour
It's the first thing you see
No longer a person
No more than a she
A once bright light
Dulled without her fight
Learning to give up for her safety
In here you best be hasty.

I am only a colour
It's the only thing you'll let me be
How come I can't be me?
Never the enemy but always a soldier
Could these views get any older?
I'm done with this war
I'm waiting for my moment
Watch me, I'll soar.

I am never only a colour
I am the power it gives me
I couldn't care less if you agree
My culture is my beauty
Being me is my only duty
You are not defined by colour
Don't let that be your duller
I am more than just my colour.

Maggie Li (13)
Garnock Community Campus, Glengarnock

Christmas

Christmas is the most wonderful time of the year
If you don't like it then I don't know who you are
Christmas is the best holiday
Christmas is the most wonderful time of the year.

Some people think Christmas is the worst thing ever
'Cause they think the whole thing is fake
I thought that about it too
But then one time I heard something
And Christmas night I heard boots walking across the hall
And I got really, really excited with joy
Christmas is the most wonderful time of the year.

It's the smell of Christmas trees
The Christmas dinner
The gifts and smiles
Laughs and joy
And lots of people love it
And you should also
Christmas is the most wonderful time of the year.

Aaron Walker (12)
Garnock Community Campus, Glengarnock

School

Some might love it, some might hate it,
Some might be somewhere in-between.
I understand the need for it but I sometimes feel like a machine.
"Do your homework."
"Be on time."
"Revise for tests."
"You can't wear that."
"Get your head down."
"No, you can't go to the toilet, I know it's just an act."
"This is preparing you for Nat 5."
"It will only get more challenging."
I'm anxious, and for free time I find myself scavenging.
I've put in my brain that anything less than 83% is unacceptable.
I don't give myself breaks but maybe, just maybe...
Good qualifications could be injectable.

Emma Galloway (13)
Garnock Community Campus, Glengarnock

The Sea

The sea, it's such a pity,
She is so dirty with oil and filth,
It's covering the fantastic fish,
How I wish I could clean her,
She's simply too big for a one-man job.

Her hair has plastic weaved into her locks,
Her eyes have lost the vibrance they had before.
The fish, they can barely breathe,
With plastic weaved in-between their gills.

Some people might disagree
But they don't know what lies below the surface.
Plastic takes hundreds of years to disintegrate,
But if you recycle and don't empty waste
You can save our beloved sea.

Save our lovely sea before it's too late.
Try and recycle waste
And don't dump it in the sea.

Kara Wotherspoon (12)
Garnock Community Campus, Glengarnock

Christmas Is The Best

Christmas time is the best time of year,
Let me tell you why...
All the joy, all the toys,
All the Christmas love!
All the snow, all the glow.
The lights are so bright, it's such a delight!
Seeing my family and obviously opening the most fantastic
presents always brings me joy.
The most fantastic countdown to Christmas makes me so,
so, so excited.
I honestly don't understand how some people don't love
Christmas.
Everything is just so beautiful and bright.
Don't get me started on Christmas decorations!
Putting up my Christmas tree is just the start of the whole
Christmas season!
The snow is falling
And the lights are glowing!

Amy Urquhart (11)
Garnock Community Campus, Glengarnock

Why?

Human, prey or predator?
So small and fragile,
Yet powerful and greedy.
We build cities and planes
But at what cost?

But we hide behind screens,
Not seeing the truth,
Where we kill an animal just for one tooth.
We've killed and poached to extinction
Or endangered ivory for a little decoration,
Tiger fur and skin for a rug.
What is the need?

But that's not all!
No, no, no!
Forests are burning,
Ice is melting at an alarming rate!
But what are we doing?
Nothing.

Dear 2035,
I don't think we're going to survive.
It's now or never.
But please...
Be better.

Mya Brown (13)
Garnock Community Campus, Glengarnock

Someone I Used To Know

Asking how I see myself is like asking a blind man how the world might look.
I see someone I don't know,
I once saw a happy woman now it's like I'm a fish on a hook,
Separated by my value,
Which one of us is dumb enough to fall for it?
A blonde would be one of their guesses.
Just for a moment of validation, for my soul to get slit,
Last night I tore and soaked a résumé with tears
Because being told a woman couldn't do it was one of my greatest fears.
I screamed and I cried,
But I covered all the marks the next day,
I handed in my sheet just to wait for them to say,
"It wasn't a woman's job."

Jessica Mitchell (12)
Garnock Community Campus, Glengarnock

Horses

Why do we starve and beat them?
It's not fair that we kill them for not winning every race they do.
Why do we treat them like slaves?
They're your partner,
You are meant to treat them kindly like you should
And some people act like they are cars
Expecting them to listen and do everything they should.
They get blamed if you fall or mess up,
Even just not coming first place in a race
Is like getting a death penalty.
A horse is your partner not your slave.
Sometimes they have up and down days.
Listen to them, love them,
Give them treats when they do good.
Help them.
Learn.
Love them like you should.

Carys Horsburgh
Garnock Community Campus, Glengarnock

Christmas Is The Best Time Of The Year

Christmas is the best time of the year,
It spreads lots of cheer.
The baubles and bells, crackers and cakes,
That's what makes it great.
Christmas is the best time of the year.

You may think it's cold and dreary
But oh, the snow makes me cheery.
Family and friends laughing all night,
Stuffing their faces with such delight.
Christmas is the best time of the year.

When the conical pine goes up for Christmas time
It gives me a festive fever.
The different shapes and sizes of gifts on the floor,
Intrigue me more and more.
Christmas is the best time of the year.

Lucy Graham (12)
Garnock Community Campus, Glengarnock

Stop Animal Abuse

Animal abuse is illegal and abusive.
Kept in cages, starved and shackled.
Cruel and abusive, these people need to be gone.
They have to, no choice.

Animals are machines, they're fine.
They don't care, they're emotionless things.
I don't care, I'll abuse them to death.
Let's leave this one,
We'll abuse something else.

Animals are not machines, stop it!
They are so horrible and abusive
They'd take their baby away.
And when you leave it I'll save it
And you'll go to jail anyway.

Kristin
Garnock Community Campus, Glengarnock

Learning To Swim = Important

Did you know...
Learning to swim is important?
It is! Because you don't want to drown do you?
No one ever wants to drown.
Learning to swim is important.

You might be thinking
You would still be able to drown!
That's true...
But you would be more likely to save yourself!
Learning to swim is important.

That's not all you would be able to do!
You could go to water parks,
Go down crazy water slides
Or swim in the sea!
"There might be sharks in the sea!"
You would be able to swim away!
Learning to swim is important.

Abigail McNaught (12)
Garnock Community Campus, Glengarnock

Lily My Love

Lily my love, I know you see me
With your dark brown chocolate eyes.
Lily my love, oh how your hair sits perfectly
Even when you don't try.
Lily my love, even if you don't love me back
Always know that you are the love of my life.
Lily my love, I know you see me with your glossy eyes,
Looking at the ring shining in the sun.
Lily my love, you said yes!
I know how happy we will be in the future.
Lily my love, you look beautiful in that white dress.
Lily my love, I know you see me standing in front of you
Looking at you with love written all over my face.

Ellie Blackwood (13)
Garnock Community Campus, Glengarnock

A Day From My Perspective

Our home is a dying mess
Thinking we have ruined it all
The beauty and kind-hearted nature
Has turned into an ugly, polluted monster

Humanity is to be blamed
The Earth isn't to be blamed
Earth did nothing wrong

Trashing and building more and more
Is not a sight to be behold
I personally think we must change this habit
We all do, us kids do
What feels like good and the right habit

This planet is gone
Except the plastic stays here
But we disappear.

Abigail O'Hara (13)
Garnock Community Campus, Glengarnock

Make A Change

This is such a disgrace,
We're leaving litter all over the place,
Spread across our streets like glitter,
It really makes me feel bitter.

Please, just throw it in the bin,
I promise it'll only take a min,
The amount of people that dump it on the floor,
Together we need to do more.

Thank you, you've helped us make a change,
Even if the end goal still isn't quite in range,
Try and change the thoughts of others,
We can do this, my sisters and brothers.

Austin Bell (13)
Garnock Community Campus, Glengarnock

Is Life Pointless?

Life is pointless
No one ever says that
Sure, everything has meaning
But it's still fact.
No matter our riches,
No matter our upbringing
We're all the same
But we still judge others,
Some people have a massive ego,
Some people always have a reason to go,
Some people are just plain rude,
Some people are constantly on the move,
Nothing is great or perfect,
That may be true,
Unless we're optimistic.

Now read from bottom to top.

Grace Willman-Howitt (12)
Garnock Community Campus, Glengarnock

No Hope, Only Despair

Pretend to be alive while marching towards death,
That's life isn't it?
That's life,
I'm broken,
I'm covered in invisible wounds
And I know that.

I don't know anything,
I don't want to know anything,
There's no deeper meaning,
Behind these words
Anyway.

Was the act of being born
A mistake?
There's no hope
In a life like this,
So I'm just standing here
In this nightmare covered in despair.

Ellie Jamieson (12)
Garnock Community Campus, Glengarnock

Dogs' Love

D ogs bring love into your life, they make your world bright.

O utside and in, they show you love if you show the same in return.

G ood or bad, they still love and would give you their life.

S nuggles you in bed makes you smile every day.

L ots of kisses to be expected.

O n walks you will play for hours as the sun goes down.

V ery special furry friends, always by your side.

E very laugh, every smile, your friend will be the reason.

Elle Carr

Garnock Community Campus, Glengarnock

Patience Is Key

Determination could get you a reward,
Giving up could cost you an opportunity,
Things might not affect you with a positive mindset,
Keep moving even if your legs fall off,
It takes too long to get a reward,
It's too hard sometimes,
Lots of bad things happen in life,
A ton of things can stop you,
That's why you should be determined,
You won't achieve anything if it's not hard,
If you think positive issues may not affect you
Keep pushing through it.

Scott Conlan (13)
Garnock Community Campus, Glengarnock

I Love Halloween

Halloween is spooky, it makes me want to boogie
Tricks and treats, ghosts and goblins
I love Halloween
You might not like it
It's scary and cold
But let me tell you
It's the best time of the year
Free sweets and dressing up
Leaves everywhere and spooky spirits coming to town
I love Halloween
I'm stuffed with sweets and treats
And I'm ready for some sleep
To dream of the spooky, spectacular night I've had
I love Halloween.

Lilli McIntyre (12)
Garnock Community Campus, Glengarnock

Flowers

Flowers are stunningly coloured.
Most of them smell like you are in Heaven.
When you think of flowers
Does summer jump into your head?

I hate flowers because I have extremely bad hay fever.
It's a complete waste of time if people destroy them.
It gets very dirty when you plant them.

Take some antihistamines for hay fever.
Planting can be a fun way to spend time with family
and friends.
Wear gardening gloves if it gets dirty.

Jessica Miller
Garnock Community Campus, Glengarnock

Guinea Pig

Guinea pigs are very intelligent
They can be fun to be with
Can be very loving to you and trustworthy
Guinea pigs are cute.

Argh! They are always noisy
They just want to eat all the time
They are stinky
And they are so messy.

No, no, no!
Guinea pigs are mostly quiet
They just love food just like us
Piggies don't smell
They are well
Guinea pigs aren't that messy
They just like having fun.

Rebecca Kirkcaldy
Garnock Community Campus, Glengarnock

Football

F ootball is the best sport ever.

O ver the world football is played and enjoyed.

O ut of 7.9 billion people 4.3 billion watched the World Cup.

T he sport is intense, you have to work hard.

B all games are played but football is the best.

A ll the continents, South America produces the best players.

L oved. Football is loved all over the world.

L oving the game, the sport brings us fans together.

James Welsh (11)
Garnock Community Campus, Glengarnock

LGBTQ+

L esbian people can hang around with girls.

G ay people can hang around with girls and wear make-up.

B isexual people can hang around with both genders.

T rans people can be whoever they want to be.

Q ueer people can be whatever they want.

'It's just a phase, they will grow out of it'.
It isn't a phase, they can be what they want.
You can't decide who they should or shouldn't be.

Keira Robertson
Garnock Community Campus, Glengarnock

Wicked Weather

When you look out the window
To see the sun shining
You begin to turn that frown upside down
You jump up and down, celebrating
The sun is back in town.

The weather can make the plants grow high
Even though the rain will cancel your plans
Just remember it helps nature
It can make your day better.

Even though it's flooded
And you can't get out of town
You can sit around and watch a family movie.

Sienna Cook (12)
Garnock Community Campus, Glengarnock

Trees

Trees are tall
Trees are shady
They give you oxygen
They're home to birds.

Trees can fall down
Trees should get chopped down
They can start forest fires
They will just fall down if they die.

If they fall down they will grow back
They should not get chopped down
Because people should not be setting forest fires
Then there wouldn't be any
You need to buy seeds for them to grow back.

Mia Armstrong
Garnock Community Campus, Glengarnock

Christmas

Christmas is pants, jumpers and Nike socks.
So you think I don't like it?
No, I do!
I was saying I get pants, jumpers and Nike socks
for Christmas.
It's my favourite time of the year
Especially to get into the Christmas spirit,
when we put our beautiful angel on the top
and watch movies in bed.
My favourite Christmas pudding is Chocolate cake
with a cherry on top
and that's why I love Christmas.

Ocean Cherry (12)
Garnock Community Campus, Glengarnock

Tell Us Why

Tell us why...
Air pollution causes 11.65% of death globally.
Tell us why...
The average waste sent to landfill from the UK is 14 million tonnes.
Tell us why...
Poverty in Britain is as high as ever.
Tell us why...
Unemployment in Britain is the most since the 80s.
Tell us why...
Inflation is as high as 2008.
Tell us why...
Nothing is being done about any of this.
Are we just livestock to the UK?

Calum Conway (13)
Garnock Community Campus, Glengarnock

Football Is A Wonderful Game

Football is full of fun,
Football is a game you run,
Football is full of fame,
Football is a wonderful game.

Football is very dull,
Especially when it ends nil-nil,
If your team's losing it isn't very joyful,
Football is not a wonderful game.

Football is full of passion,
Football can be full of tension,
Football, you need perfect aim,
Football is a wonderful game!

Roxi Baxter (12)
Garnock Community Campus, Glengarnock

Dogs

Dogs like to look after their masters.
Dogs start to smell if you don't wash them regularly.
They are adorable when they're puppies.
They get fleas if you don't give them treatment.
They love to go on walks, to run about.
Good dogs don't bark all the time.
They calm you down if you're upset.
Trained dogs don't destroy your stuff.

Bree Lepick
Garnock Community Campus, Glengarnock

On The Streets

They look down and their shoulders sag
While you walk by with your million-dollar bag.
They see people go by,
They're begging for help
And when you ignore them
It's like a big skelp!
"But I can't end homelessness,
What can I do?"
You aid them and be their voice
Because they would too!

Luisa De Stefano (12)
Garnock Community Campus, Glengarnock

Dogs

Dogs like to protect their owners.
Dogs are destructive
But dogs aren't destructive if they're trained properly.
They smell
But they won't smell if you wash them.
Dogs are cute when they're puppies
But when they get fleas you need to put cream on them.
They bark but you can train them not to bark.

Stella Smith (11)
Garnock Community Campus, Glengarnock

What Has Happened?

What has happened to this world?
A place where everyone could have their own identity
But everyone thinks they need to be a certain way
You need to like football or rugby
Kids as young as ten swear and are dirty-minded
Let kids play games and have fun
Let kids have a childhood
They won't always have that!

Charlotte Adair (12)
Garnock Community Campus, Glengarnock

Why I Love Flowers

I love flowers because...
They are very colourful and beautiful,
They also smell amazing!
There are hundreds of different kinds
And they all look different.
You can get real or fake ones
To make your home or garden more colourful.
That's why I love flowers.

Katie Neill (12)
Garnock Community Campus, Glengarnock

Sea Animals

Sea animals are helpful to us
They come and take care of our planet
But all this rubbish and waste
It is hurting our animals
We need to stop this
Animals can save us one day
Please just listen
Save our animals
Save our animals
Please do it for us!

Calum Robson (12)
Garnock Community Campus, Glengarnock

Football

F riends are all together

O n the pitch.

O ld ball and muddy grass

T hat didn't matter.

B asketball is better

A ll of them said.

L ots of people enjoy the game.

L ovely football is the best once again.

Zac Evans

Garnock Community Campus, Glengarnock

This Old Tree

The tree stands tall
Rocking back and forth in the winter wind
Branches, nothing but bare
From far away, to up close
This wise tree
Is nothing but old
From glorious summers to harsh winters
This old tree
Still stands tall.

Ailsa Macfarlane
Garnock Community Campus, Glengarnock

Birds

Birds are a beautiful thing
Every morning I listen to the ring
Some people may like them
And some people may not
But birds to me,
They are one of the most beautiful things
And every morning I listen to their ring.

Rachel Rankin (12)
Garnock Community Campus, Glengarnock

Cats

Cats!
They make the best pets.
They love to run and play.
You might think, cats?
Urgh! Never!
But do not forget,
Cats are the best!

Liam Cunningham (11)
Garnock Community Campus, Glengarnock

Fight For Animal Rights

Killing birds just for sport and for fun,
Using cattle and horses to pull carts along.

Stand up for the dogs, the cats and the birds,
Stand up for the packs, the flocks and the herds.

Cutting down trees just to build new shops.
What about the creatures living in the treetops?

Stand up for the dogs, the cats and the birds,
Stand up for the packs, the flocks and the herds.

Destroying the places animals live in,
To build stuff that will end up in the bin.

Stand up for the dogs, the cats and the birds,
Stand up for the packs, the flocks and the herds.

Keeping them all locked up in a zoo,
They live on this Earth just like me and you.

Stand up for the dogs, the cats and the birds,
Stand up for the packs, the flocks and the herds.

It's true we eat them just to survive
But that doesn't mean they can't have rights.

Rufus Higgins (12)
Looe Community Academy, East Looe

Greed Of War

Greed is a disease
A cause of conflict
For those with power will want more
Abuse their power to get more land, money, weapons and people
All they see is dollar signs piling high
But all we see is a fool looking for more than one man needs in a lifetime
No soldiers fight for their leaders but for their family
No soldiers fight for greed but for their home
A peaceful home with green grass and water flowing
Now a conflict in the field with bodies piled high, and no hope showing
To flee your home for one man's dream
A nightmare for others
The rattles of guns, the boom of bomb barricades
Witness to death
Never forget yet always want to
Soldiers fight, fight for a fool with no intent of getting his hands dirty
Discrimination and control is a product of war
Leave your family to obey the drafting law
To die in a war that is not yours
Greed is war's only cause.

Reid Hopkins (12)
Looe Community Academy, East Looe

Body Image

In the life of a teenager,
There are many people getting told what their appearance should be like.
Why are you so skinny?
You should eat something.
Why does your body look like that?
That would be the normal questions that they would hear every single day.
In their mind they would think that they're not good enough
And that they need to change.
They feel scared and alone
And that no one cares about them.
Why do people do this?
Why do people think that they can say what people should look like?
People are getting bullied and told time and time again how they should look.
It's their body,
Their mind,
They should be the ones thinking about their body image.

Sophia Williams (12)
Looe Community Academy, East Looe

Our Corrupt World

People get tortured every day,
Imagine doing that just for your payday.
People do not deserve this discrimination,
Everyone needs to drop their imagination
And live life in our corrupt creation.
Open your eyes and what do you see?
Our world falling to our feet,
Our trees falling into the deep,
Our animals experiencing their final heartbeat
Whilst we sit around and watch TV,
Watching people desperate to eat.
It's time to make a change whilst we still have a chance.
Make the world a better place
Before the next generation experiences the world's fate.
I'm ready to make a change, are you with me?

Michael Caddy (12)
Looe Community Academy, East Looe

Bullying

Bullying.
Bullying is something in our society that is known yet no one
takes action.
I find it odd: the fact people don't do anything,
They know it happens yet no one does anything,
I find it odd the fact all ages are made fun of,
I find it odd that people accept it,
I find it odd people go home and judge themselves
But we are all human after all.

People look at themselves, accepting their comments
And begin asking themselves...
What if I had a different weight?
A different height?
A different face?
What if I was someone different?
We all accept this.
But we are all human.
Bullying.

Sophie Haywood (13)
Looe Community Academy, East Looe

Climate Change Is The Concern

We need to start recycling today,
In order for our future to be okay,
Tonnes of plastic, thrown into the sea,
All wildlife in the sea:
Just let them be,
Even the factories are ruining our fresh air,
Soon we will have helmets to breathe,
So just calm down on pollution,
Then we can live our happy lives.

Think of your kids in 10 or 20 years' time,
They won't be able to see the beautiful life,
The polar bears,
They are stuck on ice,
Floating into the ocean,
Let's plan it.
To save our planet
And end this terrible plastic reign,
In order to save our fantastic African plain.

Rocky Reason (12)
Looe Community Academy, East Looe

Men Can Speak Too

Men's mental health matters,
Just as much as anyone else's,
They can speak
And not close their beaks
Just because they think they have to be strong.
If something's bad, speak out,
Don't let it get so horrible that it's unbearable,
Because then you'll lose that battle,
By yourself you'll crumble,
Others can help if you stumble,
You're not the only one,
There are people out there to talk to,
They'll help you out,
So men, speak out.

Your voice is powerful,
It can travel far and wild,
So tell someone about what's putting stress on your mind.

Archie Chainey-Smith (12)
Looe Community Academy, East Looe

Canine Chaos

It's dark in here
Screaming in my last ear
Grime in my hair
The light at the top of the stairs
It's dark in here.

I want to feel love
The devil is above me
The sun is coming up
But I can't see
I want to run

It's dark in here
Sitting in my filth
My heart that's still
Can't stand up
Won't have the life
I've dreamt of.

Can't eat
My last bowl
It's dark in here.

Now I can't feel it anymore
I can see the sun
Now I'm not the lonely one
There's light here.

Cerys Vickery (12)
Looe Community Academy, East Looe

Our Earth

Pollution, pollution, pollution,
Please stop, it hurts,
It's killing me, and all animals that live on me,
I am the Earth, the place you call home,
And you are destroying me, all the beauty I've given you,
The breathable air, the sea, water, land,
However, I get nothing in return except...
Buildings, poisoned waters and air,
Dead bodies implanted into me,
You are all a virus, like corona was to you,
What would happen if I disappeared, hmm?
You would all be helpless,
All alone
Just... like...
Me.

Evie Pearson-Roselle (12)
Looe Community Academy, East Looe

Things Are Costing Too Much

Things are costing too much,
We should take them down a touch.

Shampoo needed for people's hair,
Prices need to be reduced there.

Football shirts, also football boots,
£100! Go back to the pricing roots.

Gas and electric is costing a load,
And fuel for our cars on the road.

The gap in society is widening even more,
Some people are being forced, right out of their doors.

The poorest are struggling, they cannot cope,
Just hanging on, but they are losing hope.

Thurston Rich (12)
Looe Community Academy, East Looe

That One Person

The one person
We all hate,
They sit there with a pen in their hair
And stare at you like they don't care.
They're short and blond,
Annoying and idiotic,
Their annoying habits bore me.

That one person
That scrunches his bottle
And rhymes "Dom likes dogs",
They're only there for one lesson
But it's still bad.

So I write this poem
To those who feel the same,
Don't worry about it,
It's only Monday.

Zachary Underhill (12)
Looe Community Academy, East Looe

WWI

WWI is a deadly place,
From bombs, gunfire and sickness.
The gunfire mowing down everything in its way,
The terrible trenches bring trench foot and other illnesses.

WWI is a deadly place,
Bombs falling all around me
And gas chokes out the trenches,
The smell of all dead things fills the air
Which makes me want to die.

WWI is a deadly place,
The deafening bombs, gas attacks,
Sickness will be hard to forget
After the war if we survive.

Sam Honey (12)
Looe Community Academy, East Looe

School

That one feeling,
That one chance,
To get out of that one place
And that place is school.
That one chance is at the end of the day,
That one feeling is knowing it's Friday.
All around the world children run free,
To do what they want,
But only one thing can ruin it,
That is the end of the weekend.
Kids on Sunday oblivious
But the feeling that you know
Monday is coming
And a new 'prison' life starts,
Can you survive?

Dominic Juleff (12)
Looe Community Academy, East Looe

My Nan

My nan is the best,
You won't convince me otherwise.
Many, many nans I've seen
And let me tell you why,
My nan is the best.

You might think, is she though?
But you will think otherwise.
When you hear what she does
You will ask, why?
But my nan is the best.

The burst of joy,
The sweet, creamy milkshake,
There's no one like her,
My nan is the best.

Brandon Sibley (12)
Looe Community Academy, East Looe

Climate Change

The world is shaking
As our oceans are breaking.
The woods are burning
And the ice caps are yearning
For cooler air waves
And happier colder days.
How did they happen?
How do I help stop this thing?
So many questions
And so little time to save
Our planet from death.
The great world is heating up.
Why?
Climate change.

Gabriel Gutierrez (13)
Looe Community Academy, East Looe

Changing Seasons

Winter is cold with snow on the trees.
Cold winter nights and warm woollen mittens.
Rivers are frozen in time and animals stay inside.
The smell of cinnamon cookies is everywhere
And Christmas is here.
But when the snow melts away
All of the flowers come out,
All baby animals are scattered about.
The days are getting warmer.

Lilia Jackson (12)
Looe Community Academy, East Looe

Brilliant Person, Negative Thoughts

Bullying hurts,
The words banging your brain,
Emotions clashing with thought,
It hurts, doesn't it?
Open up, it doesn't help,
Close down, it will hurt,
Why hasn't this stopped?
Why do they feel as if they have to suffer in silence?
This shouldn't happen,
Let's end bullying
One word at a time.

Adam Courtenay (12)
Looe Community Academy, East Looe

Summer

Summer.
Heatwaves,
Picnics,
Lazy days.
Happiness,
No stress about school.
Parties,
Eating Smarties,
No school!
Beach walks,
Swimming in the sea.
Dressing up.
Having fun with friends.
Sleepovers!
Going to bed late.
Sleeping in,
Ice cream!
Summer is the best time of year!

Kara Mark (12)
Looe Community Academy, East Looe

Autumn

Autumn is coming
Leaves falling all over the floor
Halloween is here.

Colours everywhere
Dressing up all through the night
Kids knocking on doors.

Pumpkins are coming
And sweets all through the next day
Summer is all over.

Leah Chalk (13)
Looe Community Academy, East Looe

The North Pole

The ice is melting,
There once were polar bears dancing on ice,
But now polar bears are drowning in water,
Starving to death,
Living on land.
This is dangerous for all of us,
So let's do something about it.

George Dickens (12)
Looe Community Academy, East Looe

My Daily Life

I wake up, I look up to the ceiling to see spiral designs
dancing in the sunlight.
I get up, I go downstairs and greet my parents with their
eyes shining and twinkling almost like there's a star.
I brush my teeth, eat breakfast and get dressed.
I head out in the car, the engine roars as the car starts up.
As we drive past trees, bushes, pigs and farms,
I look at the droplets on the window slowly moving down,
Like us getting further and further away from home.
I think of the hard subjects in school,
But I push myself not to worry and keep going.
As I reach the school, I say goodbye to my beloved parents
and off I go to find my friends.
As I wait for the gate to open, I shiver as the breezy wind
zooms by like a NASCAR.
I go into my first class, I sit down, doing the 'do now' task.
After a few lessons, it's break time, I sit down and wait for
my next lesson.
As the time flies by it is already hometime.
I reach home, eat dinner and play some games.
I have a shower, go up to my bed and tuck in.
And that is my daily life, goodnight.

Anson Wong (11)
Sybil Andrews Academy, Bury St Edmunds

The Future Of Technology

T echnology plays a massive part in the future of our planet.

E nergy. New technology will have to be more energy efficient in the future.

C ar charging points. Electric cars need more charging points to become a 'big thing' in the UK.

H ydrogen power is becoming more popular which will help us to achieve a net zero future.

N ew technology. We have to get new technology that is energy efficient into the shops and persuade people to buy them.

O ld technology. When we are disposing of our old non-energy-efficient equipment we should do it responsibly to save our planet.

L overs of technology. Lovers of technology like me know how important new technology is to saving our planet.

O ther countries. We all work together to develop groundbreaking energy-efficient technologies.

G oals. If we all try to reach the goal of energy-efficient equipment we could help save the planet.

Y our future technology. Your new technology will be more energy efficient, so you can help save the planet too!!

Olly Ramsbottom (11)

Sybil Andrews Academy, Bury St Edmunds

The Journey Of IShowSpeed And Bullying

Speed is a YouTuber, he thinks Ronaldo's the GOAT!
If I could write how many times he has scored,
I would need a bigger note.
Speed is a legend, he is my lad,
Some say he's crazy, but he's not that bad.

He is great, he is someone I admire,
Even though on 4th July, he started a fire.
Speed is flying up the YouTube chart, fast as The Flash,
And being a YouTuber is big,
And you get a lot of cash.

Even Speed is bullied online, for how weird he is,
But he ignores it and carries on with his life,
That you can't miss.
If you are also bullied online, and it makes you sad,
Go tell a trusted adult, such as your mum or dad.

Speed shows the world that when you're being bullied,
Ignore it and be who you are.
Carry on with your life, and see if you can go far.
Some bullies might not be bad, they just have a bad life,
Just think about your future, with your future husband or
wife.

George Kydd (12)
Sybil Andrews Academy, Bury St Edmunds

Flashback

The horrors of war,
The horrors of fire,
The horror of police sirens,
Your mind starts to tire.

They give service to this country,
For the freedom of you and me,
The scary part is,
It's an illness we cannot see.

The lives that I took,
Said to be in vain,
Now I look back,
And all I see is pain.

A wound that lies deep,
Far, far within,
They call me weak
If I cry for my sins.

Blue and red lights,
Flashing from colour to colour,
I've turned up to something,
My memories will get duller.

The body bag is zipped,
And so are my emotions,

Numbed were my feelings,
The death, the commotion.

George Rowson (13) & Charlie

Sybil Andrews Academy, Bury St Edmunds

Equal Rights

People should not be forced into doing a job they don't
want to do,
People should have a choice,
People should have rights.
It doesn't matter your race,
We are all human.

Don't discriminate or be homophobic,
We are all human.

Don't be racist or bully people
Because their skin is a different colour,
We are all human no matter our race.

Don't be peer pressured,
You are who you are.
Don't let other people control you,
You are you.

For a fairer future, we must fight for it,
We can't just sit at home and let it keep going on.
We are all human no matter our race.

Aaron Baker (12)
Sybil Andrews Academy, Bury St Edmunds

Destruction

D estroying our world, that's what we're doing,
E ver since the 19th century, you see,
S ince we took a big bite, we're still chewing,
T ransforming our world, where it's a place with no glee,
R eturning to the present, we take a look at our homes,
U nder everything, we know, we are so sincerely wrong,
C ontrol everything, clean it up with some soap then some foam,
T hough if only we had peace, bang would go the gong,
I n the midst of everything, we take one last breath,
O n we go, fixing this horrid mess,
N ever I would think, we could fix everything.

Harry Fitchett (12)
Sybil Andrews Academy, Bury St Edmunds

Voice Of A Muslim

I'm not a terrorist, not cruel or evil,
I'm not a terrorist, not a criminal,
No one cares, the attention is minimal,
Why does everyone hate me?
I haven't done anything at all,
The stares, whispers and bullying in corridors,
Hiding behind doors,
Discrimination is against the law,
Haven't you heard?
Syria, Yemen, Afghanistan, and more,
We are all suffering from your wars,
We all bleed the same blood, cry the same tears,
Our fears are ignored,
Can't take it anymore,
We have no support,
Us Muslims are bored, us Muslims are torn,
We are not terrorists, and we deserve more.

Melisa Simsek (13)
Sybil Andrews Academy, Bury St Edmunds

Poetry Is A Super Power

T ry your best always
H elp yourself succeed
E xperiment with your poem

P ersevere through the difficult times
O vercome your fear of competitions
W rite your ideas, they are never stupid
E dit your writing
R ecognise mistakes are things that help you learn

O vercome your fear of failure
F ailure only happens when you don't try

P ush yourself to success
O vercome your fear of rhyming
E dit your poem with confidence
T ake a break
R ecognise you are powerful
Y es you are!

Hayden-Jai Ankin (12)
Sybil Andrews Academy, Bury St Edmunds

Save Our One And Only Planet!

E arth is our planet, it's slowly dying.
N ow is your time to save this Earth!
V isualise our dying world
I nvading the Earth are our buried plastics.
R ain now falls harder than it ever did.
O zone layers burning slowly away.
N ow is the time to stop your littering!
M other Earth needs our help.
E nvironmental issues need to be fixed.
N ow we need to stop hurting our planet!
T ime is ticking by, we don't have long!
A dditional helping hands will help save the Earth.
L ove our planet, it's the only one we have.

Theo Newport (12)
Sybil Andrews Academy, Bury St Edmunds

It's Time To Make A Stand

We can't just stand and watch
As the war evolves around us.
We can't just stand and watch
As families are torn apart.
We can't just stand and watch
As the bombs destroy the innocent.
We can't just stand and watch
As the pure is stolen from their hearts.

It's time to make a stand
With the Russians that are in the wrong.
It's time to make a stand,
With the people that scream and yelp.
It's time to make a stand,
As they hide from the ruthless soldiers.
It's time to make a stand,
They really need our help.

Oscar Donoghue (11)
Sybil Andrews Academy, Bury St Edmunds

Our World Was Once A Whole

Our world was once a whole
From human to mole
Elephants to birds
So these words
These words may be little
But our world is getting brittle.

There are wars
With big roars
Not just rows
People prowl
Countries in destruction
Our world is dying
Nature is crying
We're hurting our own world
There is no Planet B
We're polluting everything in sight
So please help us fight.

Our world was once a whole
From human to mole
Elephants to birds
So these words

These words may be little
But our world is getting brittle.

Isabelle Dyer (12)

Sybil Andrews Academy, Bury St Edmunds

Making It To Pro

Your journey begins when you're young,
When your foot hits the ball,
You feel the passion build up within you,
And you start your journey to pro.

You play down the park with your friends,
Kicking the ball through sun, rain, mud and snow,
Watching your favourite football stars make it to pro,
You play hours and hours with family and friends
Getting better every minute and practising every day.

You join a club and build your talent,
You play through thick and thin
And win and lose but you carry on,
Through and through to make it to pro!

Woody Gresham (12)
Sybil Andrews Academy, Bury St Edmunds

Needs To Stop

Wind bursts, orange fire curtains,
Sweeping the land, fueled blazes,
There in the Arctic and Antarctic, disintegrating cuts of ice,
The size of a small country.

Sodden wreckage continues, hustling,
Disasters continue bothering,
Thrashing heatwaves and fires,
Thrashing glacial melts and storms,
Inflicting floods and climactic crashes,
Massive attacks, why?

Ozone layer depleting,
Greenhouse emissions repeating,
Causes are us, cautious we must be,
Speed of nature, can we compete?
Wish, Mother Earth is sick,
Can we curb quick?

Lewie Currington (14)
Sybil Andrews Academy, Bury St Edmunds

Cost Of Living

C hristmas is nearly here
O rnaments, decorations, so, so pricey
S hoes, clothing, why so much money?
T ime to buy more presents

O ur family's savings going towards it all
F ather Christmas has now gone broke

L ights are using all our money for electricity
I don't know how to afford it all
V alue of items so much more
I nviting everyone for Xmas and I have to pay for it
N ever stop shopping
G iving them all my money, why can't things go back to normal prices?

Sienna Lionnet-Cook (11)
Sybil Andrews Academy, Bury St Edmunds

Cost Of Living

We need to be grateful,
what we have might not be for others.
Family members working for money,
happiness and health.
Some people may have more than others,
this doesn't mean they are any better.

We are only human,
no one should take what they have for granted.
The amount of money you have doesn't describe you,
only you and the people you love
know you for who you are.
Respect your family for what you are given.

No matter how much money you have,
you are one of us,
we have respect
for you and your family.

Phoebe Harden (11)
Sybil Andrews Academy, Bury St Edmunds

Saving The Environment

Don't destroy trees,
Save the animals like bees,
Save the animals' homes
Who burrow in holes.

Who live in the underground,
Who can hear a lot of sound,
Muzzling sounds from everywhere
And the sound of a rattling chainsaw appears.

But wait, the lack of oxygen,
The world can't live without.
Every day we can breathe in and out,
Until we can't.

The animals scattered away
So the people cut their homes down,
Nobody can stop them, it's too late now,
We'll try to stop them next time.

Freya Halls (11)
Sybil Andrews Academy, Bury St Edmunds

Old Memories

O ver the bridge was a duck pond.
L ovely green grass and bright blue skies.
D aisies all over and ducks waiting for bread.

M y granny laughed in the sun as we had lot of fun.
E ating my bacon roll as the ducks quacked.
M y marvellous McCoy's were crunchy and sweet.
O range peel scattered over the ground.
R ising up throwing some tasty bread.
I n a second the ducks were up and eating.
E very moment we had I enjoyed.
S ad memories stay with you forever.

Megan Edley (11)
Sybil Andrews Academy, Bury St Edmunds

Social Media - Cyberbullying Safety

S afety, of cyberbullying is very important
O nly friends should see what you post
C yberbullying could affect your well-being
I nside and out, only post to who you love most
A rguments can hurt your feelings online
L ife can be hard with hackers

M aybe consider putting posts on private
E nd cyberbullying for the love of God
D ying online can make you say crazy things
I f you get insulted, try not to bawl
A nd finally, stop cyberbullying once and for all.

Charlie Hickford (11)
Sybil Andrews Academy, Bury St Edmunds

Reintroduction?

The animals that Britain had
But are no longer left in the wild,
As soon as our generation are dads,
We want all the kids to have the luxury
Of knowing they're in an eco-country.

The wolves and bears,
The red squirrels and boars,
Send all the grey squirrels,
Home to North America.

To save the wild,
To be good to our future children,
Send all the grey squirrels
Home to North America.

To save the wild,
To be good to our future children,
To have reintroduction completed and done.

Finn Davies (11)
Sybil Andrews Academy, Bury St Edmunds

Catastrophic Climate

The world is corrupting
and the atmosphere is crumbling.
The sky is falling
and animals are stalling.
Pandas soon may not even exist,
and with the pandemic, all eyes are on it.

Everyone has forgotten about the danger
we have been facing.
Nobody has remembered the world is dying
and nobody has noticed fossil fuels are polluting,
and baby turtles are scooting
to their deaths.

Please, I'm begging you,
save the Earth.
Or, before you know it,
there will be nothing to save.

Oliver Leightley Richards (12)
Sybil Andrews Academy, Bury St Edmunds

Planet A

Fresh flowers and clear seas
What happened? you ask. Well, you will see
Factories working and people fighting
There's no Planet B
We have to act fast
No whales, no turtles, nowhere to live
Where destroying our world and future lives
The world's heating up
We will burn to crisp
If we don't do something quick
The beautiful things around us are disappearing
And here you are watching your TV
Just chilling
All I can say is
Don't come to me when your child can't breathe!

Grace Jackson (11)
Sybil Andrews Academy, Bury St Edmunds

Queen And Knight

He went out into the blinding light,
As my humble and loyal knight,
My knight is out there fighting for my kingdom,
And I stare out of my window,
Helpless.
I am the queen,
He is my knight in shining armour,
We used to play together,
Now it's now or never,
Every second without my knight is torture,
He is sacrificing his life,
For my safety,
I worry for him,
Bombs drop,
Guns fire,
Survival is everyone's focus,
I am a queen,
He is my knight,
We don't die.

Merryana Bhujel (11)
Sybil Andrews Academy, Bury St Edmunds

Save Our Oceans

P lastic is all over the ocean killing numbers of animals

O ceans are becoming unsafe for sealife

L ittering is getting out of hand

L ife for animals is hard and we are making it harder

U nder the sea pollution is taking over

T oxins in the water are killing off the sealife

I believe that if we all chip in we can save our planet

O ceans are such magical places and we need to save them

N obody should litter because it does so much damage to the world.

Lilly Farkas (11)
Sybil Andrews Academy, Bury St Edmunds

Why Waste Resources?

I look out of the window and see many rooftops
A petrol car rushes by
I see all the lamps using electricity
People wasting resources
I see the chimneys billowing smoke
The plants shrivelling up
This needs to stop.

I look out of the window and see many rooftops
A steam train rushes by
I see a busy port and boats trading cargo
I see many people playing like nothing's going on
This needs to stop.

Why are we wasting all these things?
This needs to stop.

Ethan Gatley (12)
Sybil Andrews Academy, Bury St Edmunds

Pollution's Not Allowed

The fish in the ocean,
The plastic in the sea,
Sealife dying, bottles open,
Conservation for the bees.

Fires burning, on the land,
Gases in the air,
Whales stuck on the sand,
Pandas' lives are rare.

One small change can change a lot,
Conservation for plants and wildlife,
No panda species like a dot,
No trees deserve a knife.

Equality for animals about,
Pollution not allowed,
We can change a life today,
Come along and help us out.

Alfie Turner (12)

Sybil Andrews Academy, Bury St Edmunds

Pressure

Pressured, that's how I feel,
It's just a plant, they say,
Things will feel less real.

I want to be an outcast,
I want to fit in,
It's fine, it won't last.

I start to cough, I'm asthmatic,
It doesn't take long,
I really start to panic.

I start to feel lost,
I start to feel scared,
My 'friends' still don't care.

I try to text home,
My text doesn't send,
I want this gone, I want this to end.

Rudie Lorking (13)
Sybil Andrews Academy, Bury St Edmunds

Rights

I am who I am,
I don't care if you hate me.
Whether I am black, mixed, or white,
I don't care because it's alright.
People in this world are different,
whether it is because of their gender or
if they have a different skin colour.

Autism, dyslexia, ADHD
are all different types of disabilities.
Some may be hidden,
some may be not.
We are all equal, no matter what,
If anyone says otherwise,
don't listen to them because they're not nice.

Phoebe-Mai Watts (11)

Sybil Andrews Academy, Bury St Edmunds

Discrimination

D on't be racist
I nclude everyone
S top racism
C ome together to defeat it together
R acism is not cool
I t's not too late to help
M ake our world a better place
I nclude every race
N o race is superior
A ll come together to stop it
T ell everyone to stop racism
I t's never too late to do the right thing
O ne world, many races, don't be racist
N ever be racist.

Joshua Hammond (13)
Sybil Andrews Academy, Bury St Edmunds

Stop Pollution

S ave the oceans,
T ime to act,
O nly one Earth,
P lastic kills fish.

P ollution raises CO_2 emissions.
O nly so long till we can't fix our mistakes.
L ive factories create CO_2.
L ots of traffic means lots of pollution.
U ntold damage has been done.
T ime is vital.
I n the oceans that used to be thriving, now dead.
O ur chance to act is now.
N o one could bear the end of life.

Lenny Horn (11)
Sybil Andrews Academy, Bury St Edmunds

Our Pets Matter

O utstanding creatures
U nderstanding what we say
R especting our every move for them

P recious creatures
E ither big or small
T ime with them every day
S urprising them with toys

M ostly being shoved in tiny cages
A nd never getting a healthy diet
T hey need exercise
T hey don't get that though
E ither have a pet and respect them, or don't
R espect them, please.

Faith Coston (11)

Sybil Andrews Academy, Bury St Edmunds

Our Future

F or us the future is changing
U p, no down, the world is going wrong
T urtles are experiencing a great loss
U nder our noses the world is getting polluted
R ubbish needs to be recycled
E nough, we need to make a change

F or if we do not
O ur world will be a misery
R ubbish needs to be recycled

U nder our feet trees are being chopped down
S o please help make a change and stop climate change.

Oliver Buerling (11)
Sybil Andrews Academy, Bury St Edmunds

Our Climate

Our climate is constantly changing,
It's time to stop and look at the clock,
It's still ticking,
We need to start thinking.

Think for our future,
Think for our future.

If we don't stop now our world will die,
Why not just bin your rubbish,
Now birds can't fly.
It's not our ancestors' fault,
It's ours, so let's stop and think,
Make our future better for all,
Stop now or our world will fall!

Lucas Palframan (13)
Sybil Andrews Academy, Bury St Edmunds

Fight To Save The Planet

One last chance,
One last chance to save our planet,
One last chance to save the oceans' life and colour,
One last chance to save the sky, sun, moon, clouds, and stars,
One last chance to save the land, animals, humans, and environment,
One last chance to come together,
One last fight against the beast,
One last fight against the heat,
One last fight to save the world,
One last fight to save us all,
One last fight to save it all.

Joe Harden (13)
Sybil Andrews Academy, Bury St Edmunds

LGBTQ

Whatever your sexuality,
We are all humans,
We are all living.
Sexuality doesn't change who we are,
Lesbian, gay, bisexual,
Transgender, queer,
We won't ever be the same,
But we are all humans.
No matter what, you are in the LGBTQ,
Or if you're straight, nothing changes who you are,
Stop being homophobic.
Never make someone feel down or left out
Because of the sexuality
Or the person they are.

Lauren Tee (13)
Sybil Andrews Academy, Bury St Edmunds

Yes To Respect, No To Racists

R acists are never welcome.
A t this time in the world, there should be no one to discriminate.
C hanges need to be made,
I t is not okay to take anything away from people because of their beliefs,
S tand up for what you believe,
M ake this world safe.

O n to the future we look,
U nder your own control there should be no problems,
T ogether this can be a safe planet!

Zac Horler (11)
Sybil Andrews Academy, Bury St Edmunds

War

Our world has evolved
Discrimination and any wars have been resolved
The past is stuck in history now
So why are we going back?

We are finally away from these times
Even if it's just a little bit
Someone took away their freedom
'Cause people can have the greediness of a pig.

As smoke filled their sky
While gunshots echoed in people's ears
You come to think
What happened to world peace?

Isabelle Ramsbottom (11)
Sybil Andrews Academy, Bury St Edmunds

Perfect

I am who I am,
Nobody can change me,
But there are so many rules to conform to,
So many celebrities portraying perfection,
But what is perfect?

You open your phone to see people with
The perfect life,
Perfect body,
Perfect house,
But it is not what it seems.

It's not true,
They pretend to have the perfect body,
House,
Life,
No one's life is as perfect as it seems.

Sophie Daniel (11)
Sybil Andrews Academy, Bury St Edmunds

Feel Empowered And Be Yourself!

It's not just their world - it's yours too,
Peer pressure may be too much for you.
Don't feel unempowered and that you can't be yourself,
Nor don't worry about your wealth.

Bullying is too much to take in
And you may feel like you belong in a bin,
But you don't,
And you won't.

There is one more thing you need to remember,
This world was made for everyone!

Layla Owen (12)
Sybil Andrews Academy, Bury St Edmunds

Pollution Has To Stop

We are ruining our world,
Destroying the future,
Refusing every chance we get to save our planet,
Bush fires crackling, every step of the way,
What can we do to help our home?

Pick up litter,
Fight the bitter,
Walk to school,
Don't fill up the fuel.

Start from scratch,
Erase all of our bad acts,
Together we can do this,
Let's fight for what's right!

Marie Lebrun (11)
Sybil Andrews Academy, Bury St Edmunds

I Want To Be A Footballer

The future is in your hands
Identity, what we love
Mindset, work hard
And listen up.

Regrets, dropping off, junk food
Not enough working out
I want to be a footballer
I want to shine out.

I train every day
But things still don't go my way
No time to sit around
The clock is still ticking around.

I want to be a footballer
I want to shine out.

Riley Parker (12)
Sybil Andrews Academy, Bury St Edmunds

Racism In Football

R acism isn't a good thing and should be stopped forever
A nd Saka shouldn't get abused because he missed a pen'
in the final, there's a World Cup in two months
C onquering the world and it's making people from
different races unhappy
I nappropriate - this isn't what we want in the world
S uicidal, that's why it should stop
M ake it stop!

Olly Rolfe
Sybil Andrews Academy, Bury St Edmunds

Magical Sea Creatures

A t the bottom of the sea
T here lies...
L inguens
A nd
N irdige.
T hey couldn't stop fighting,
I rritating each other.
C ollided together.

O range octopuses were made.
C onnected together.
E arth ends disappeared
A nd orange octopuses took over.
N ow we have orange octopuses.

Maja Wazydrag (11)
Sybil Andrews Academy, Bury St Edmunds

Sexist Hate

S exist hate

E quality. Let's get the meaning straight

X enophobia. We are women not strangers, we do not deserve hate

I t's not a debate

S orry isn't enough

T his has got to stop

H as the world gone blind?

A t this moment we'll find

T he world is miserable

E verybody's sadness is not risky.

Poppy Moore (11)
Sybil Andrews Academy, Bury St Edmunds

Minecraft World

M ining in my Minecraft world.

I n my super Minecraft base.

N ever ever die to Minecraft creepers.

E very night, every day, Minecraft all the way.

C an I find some diamonds in this cave?

R eeling in my fishing rod.

A creeper killed my pet Minecraft mob.

F ailed to kill the Ender Dragon.

T his Minecraft world is just too hard.

Henry Heath (12)

Sybil Andrews Academy, Bury St Edmunds

In The Future

In the future, there could be flying cars,
There could also be people going to Mars,
People could be turning into robots
And people could be going crazy,
While others will be sitting down being lazy,
And others will be playing football outside, having fun,
And people could go on a run.

People up on Mars could be floating around,
And others would have a walk around.

William Ainger (11)
Sybil Andrews Academy, Bury St Edmunds

Netball Therapy

N etball is my therapy, whenever I am sad.

E very night I dream about being on the England netball team.

T he escape I need after school;

B ecause I get so happy when I get the ball!

A t 10 when we start to play, in my head I scream, "Yay!"

L ove the feeling when I score a goal.

L ove it even more when we win the game!

Ava Whelan (12)

Sybil Andrews Academy, Bury St Edmunds

Let's Help Save The Environment

Fish are happy little creatures,
They don't deserve to die.
If we don't stop littering then many more fish will die
And soon the ocean will be covered in rubbish.
Let's help save the environment,
Let's not destroy our planet.
We were born and raised on it,
Let's have some respect for the world
And to the lovely animals that live on it too.

Sophia Saunders (11)
Sybil Andrews Academy, Bury St Edmunds

Littering The Earth

L ittle bits of litter around every corner

I think it gets addictive

T otally cool, right? (I'm being sarcastic)

T oo much rubbish on this planet

E ra to era, rubbish piles get bigger

R ubbish is building up

I might not be strong but I want this world to be clean

N o one uses bins

G et the job done.

Holly Allen (11)
Sybil Andrews Academy, Bury St Edmunds

Life Itself

The world is full
The world is life
The world has problems
The world has war
The world has good and bad
Help to change the bad.

Life is fair
Life is unfair
Life is everything
Life is everywhere
Karma is written in the rules of life
Help change it for the better.

You can't change the past
But help change our future.

Ollie Richardson (11)
Sybil Andrews Academy, Bury St Edmunds

Friendship

Friendship.
Friends should be kind and nice to you.
Friends should look out for you.
Stand up for you.
Friends should have fun with you
And laugh with you.
Friends should share with you
And never leave you out.
Friends should be honest with you
Even if sometimes it's hard.
And lastly, friends should always be there for you
No matter what.

Emelia Roe (12)
Sybil Andrews Academy, Bury St Edmunds

Autumn Feelings

A utumn is a season with crunchy orange leaves.
U mbrellas are used when it rains.
T rees become bare as all the leaves fall to the ground.
U nder trees, hiding from the pouring rain.
M inuscule mushrooms glow in the grass.
N ature surrounds you on long, drizzly walks.

This is what the future should be like.

William Johnston (12)

Sybil Andrews Academy, Bury St Edmunds

Loopy Liz Truss

L ower income tax for the poor not the rich
I feel that she is just an annoying itch
Z ero care for the UK

T hey won't make it to next May
R ishi Sunak should have won
U nder Liz Truss we'll all be done
S o much focus on imported cheese
S o little care to put the public at ease.

Alex Robb (13)
Sybil Andrews Academy, Bury St Edmunds

Football

F ootball is a lovely sport and fun to play
O f course, it's your choice if you want to
O nly if you like football and want to
T o be able to you need to know the basics
B ack at the goal is the goalkeeper
A t the front is a striker
L eft is left-wing
L ime green is the colour of grass.

Travis Hope (12)
Sybil Andrews Academy, Bury St Edmunds

Friends

F riends will look after you.
R eally need help in class, they will help you.
I f I am lonely, they will come.
E very day they are here, look up in the sky, they will be in the clouds.
N earby always.
D ream about them if you are sad.
S ay, "Friends!" They are nice, helpful, amazing.

Lily Cooper (11)
Sybil Andrews Academy, Bury St Edmunds

Save Us Now, Before It's Too Late

Save us now
Before it's too late
We are heading down a dangerous path
And the future isn't looking bright
Save us from the danger we may face
And all that may come
You have the power to save this world
The place we call home
Save us now
Before it's too late
Save us now
Before it's too late!

Luke Sadler (13)
Sybil Andrews Academy, Bury St Edmunds

Why?

Why do I feel like this?
Why do I look like this?
Why is my face so wonky?
Why are my teeth so yellow?
Why do I resemble a donkey?
Why am I so ugly?

Why are these girls so beautiful?
Why are these girls so perfect?
Why do these photos have this effect
that makes me feel like I'm not worth it?

Evie Clifford (13)
Sybil Andrews Academy, Bury St Edmunds

Abuse

Some humans hurt animals,
thinking it's fun,
but it's not.
Abuse can happen
while howls get louder.
Thinking he was your special boy,
what happened to the joy?
Misusing them like toys.
How would you feel?
Making you lose blood,
or shout at them every day.
They have a heart.

Alisha Moss (11)
Sybil Andrews Academy, Bury St Edmunds

Autism, Unravelling The String

A spectrum of personalities and views
U nderstanding emotional conflicts may be a struggle
T rying unique methods can help us learn easier
I n our minds, it can feel like a puzzle
S ome people may look, stare, and call us weird
M y awareness poem can be linked to one word.

Jordan Ward (13)
Sybil Andrews Academy, Bury St Edmunds

The Future

As the days go on,
our future is being destroyed
by people not putting little things
in the right bin.
One little thing adds up to
millions of bottles
floating in the sea,
litter and waste.
Some things can fly out of the window,
but littering can't.
This needs to change.

Wesley Andrade (11)
Sybil Andrews Academy, Bury St Edmunds

Save The World

S abotage
A ll
V egetable
E ating

T ogether
H elps
E veryone

W e'll
O rganise and
R ealise
L earn this and we shall overcome
D on't and we shall suffer.

Rodrigo Teixeira (11)
Sybil Andrews Academy, Bury St Edmunds

On The Cover Of Magazines

Stereotypes are not fair,
Tall and blonde with perfect hair,
Insecure people always read
Things on the cover of magazines.

People should stop being self-conscious,
Bullies need to stop being obnoxious,
People lose their self-esteem
On the cover of magazines.

Juliet Mead (13)
Sybil Andrews Academy, Bury St Edmunds

I Don't Like Poetry

P oetry is something I don't like.
O h, how much I don't want to write this.
E verything I am writing is annoying me.
T his is probably a terrible poem.
R eaders, do you like this terrible thing?
Y ay! I have finished this poem.

Sebine Westgate (12)
Sybil Andrews Academy, Bury St Edmunds

We Need To Stop Racism In Football Now!

We need to stop racism
And get it out of this world.
You need to stop racism
And help spread the word.
Racism is a disgrace,
Show people it doesn't matter your race.
Make sure it is gone, no matter the place.
We will take the knee and take it proud.

Louie Whiting (11)
Sybil Andrews Academy, Bury St Edmunds

Reduce, Reuse And Recycle

I believe we can help the ever-changing environment.
I believe we can reduce paper with scrap paper.
I believe we can reuse bottles instead of them being thrown away.
I believe we can recycle more plastic to reuse and reduce wasted plastic.
Reduce, reuse and recycle.

Riley Wall (12)
Sybil Andrews Academy, Bury St Edmunds

160

Our World, Our Planet, Our Responsibility

This world,
This planet,
The humans,
We've destroyed our home.

We have ruined it all for all the generations to come.
It's our fault,
And to fix it, it will take everyone.

Our world,
Our planet,
Our responsibility.

Henry Myhill (11)
Sybil Andrews Academy, Bury St Edmunds

We Can Change Racism

R ights. We need to have our rights and respect

A wful comments made by fans

C ompanies need to ban these types of people

I t is not okay to treat people this way

S tand up for what's right now

M ake a change.

Lily Webber (12)

Sybil Andrews Academy, Bury St Edmunds

Emotions

Sadness, all around us
Happiness, shining like a star
Anger, underneath our skin, hiding from the light
Confusion, walking around the streets.

These are our key emotions
They are all needed to go through life
Feel them when needed.

Riley Summers (11)
Sybil Andrews Academy, Bury St Edmunds

No Room For Racism

R ights to do the same things other people can.
A wful comments made by fans should be banned.
C lubs need to ban these fans.
I t's time to start noticing it.
S top being racist!
M ake a change people!

Taylor Parker (11)
Sybil Andrews Academy, Bury St Edmunds

Stop Racism

R espect all races in all sports,
A nd we don't need people who treat people in a bad way.
C ould we stop this?
I think everyone should have equal rights.
S tand up for yourself.
M ake this stop!

Louie Dobbyn (11)
Sybil Andrews Academy, Bury St Edmunds

Identity

I am me, you are you
D reams will come true
E very day I don't give up
N ever give up on yourself
T ake your time
I dentity is key
T ry new things
Y ou are loved.

Evie Roscoe (12)
Sybil Andrews Academy, Bury St Edmunds

Human Rights

Whether you are black, white, girl, boy,
They are who they are and no one can change that,
Who are you to judge them?
People should celebrate how we are all unique,
Same would be boring, being different makes us all stand out.

Erin Stewart (11)
Sybil Andrews Academy, Bury St Edmunds

War And Pain

W hen will it stop?
A n endless battle
R uins the world

P owerful and greedy leaders
A ll our lives will be ruined
I hate the suffering
N ow finish the fight.

Theo Baillie (11)
Sybil Andrews Academy, Bury St Edmunds

This Planet

This planet needs to change
But it can only change with your help.
This is all because of the rubbish in our oceans
And toxins in the air.
The planet slowly dies.
In the years to come, it will finally die.

Freddie Cole (12)
Sybil Andrews Academy, Bury St Edmunds

Winter Warmth

W arm fire roaring

I ce skating

N ature nowhere to be seen

T ucked up in bed waiting, hoping, Christmas will come soon

E ating Christmas dinner

R otting away at home.

Annie Murrell (11)

Sybil Andrews Academy, Bury St Edmunds

Anything Helps

R espect should be given to all people.
A ll skin colours are beautiful.
C an you stop staring?
I want change!
S ave me from this world.
M y race doesn't matter.

Aliona Day (11)
Sybil Andrews Academy, Bury St Edmunds

Football Power

R espect should be in all sports.
A wful comments in sports and football.
C ourage to stop this!
I t is not acceptable.
S tand up.
M ake change.

Sonni French (11)
Sybil Andrews Academy, Bury St Edmunds

Equal Rights

I want the world to have equal rights
Not in-between family fights
I would like to have justice
But right now all I see is a crisis
We should reach many heights.

Felix Glasscock (12)
Sybil Andrews Academy, Bury St Edmunds

Prices Rising

M ortgages rising too quick to manage.

O nly so much left.

N eeds to stop.

E veryone is panicking.

Y elling for help.

Mia Dallorzo (11)

Sybil Andrews Academy, Bury St Edmunds

Pollution

A haiku

This is important,
Polluters just puff out smoke,
Toxic chemicals.

Oliver Bivins (11)

Sybil Andrews Academy, Bury St Edmunds

Let's Tackle Racism Together

A haiku

I believe we can
Make a change for racism
Will you stand with me?

Lexie Proctor (11)

Sybil Andrews Academy, Bury St Edmunds

Life

L ife is like a test.
I t's complicated.
F ind the right way,
E liminate sadness and sorrow.

Franciszek Inglot (11)

Sybil Andrews Academy, Bury St Edmunds

Rugby

R eally fun
U nforgettable
G ood teamwork
B est friends
Y ummy food afterwards.

Beau Proctor (11)

Sybil Andrews Academy, Bury St Edmunds

YoungWriters®
— Est. 1991 —

YOUNG WRITERS
INFORMATION

We hope you have enjoyed reading this book – and
that you will continue to in the coming years.

If you're the parent or family member of an
enthusiastic poet or story writer, do visit our website
www.youngwriters.co.uk/subscribe and sign up to receive
news, competitions, writing challenges and tips, activities
and much, much more! There's lots to
keep budding writers motivated!

If you would like to order further copies of this book,
or any of our other titles, then please give us a
call or order via your online account.

Young Writers
Remus House
Coltsfoot Drive
Peterborough
PE2 9BF
(01733) 890066
info@youngwriters.co.uk

Join in the conversation!
Tips, news, giveaways and much more!

 **YoungWritersUK**  **YoungWritersCW**  **youngwriterscw**